What This Book Will Do for You

By the time you finish reading this book, you'll be in a better position to hire the right people to do the right jobs by designing job descriptions that zero in on the qualifications and the qualities of the person who can do the job. By talking less, asking the right—and legal—questions, and listening to the answers, you'll learn how to make rational hiring decisions. So read on. . . .

Other Titles in the Successful Office Skills Series

HOW TO BE A
Successful
Interviewer

Donald H. Weiss

amacom
American Management Association

Library of Congress Cataloging-in-Publication Data

Weiss, Donald H., 1936–
  How to be a successful interviewer.

  (The Successful office skills series)
  Includes index.
  1. Employment interviewing.   I. Title.   II. Series.
HF5549.5.I6W45   1988   658.3'1124   88-47698
ISBN 0-8144-7697-X

Printing Number

10 9 8 7 6

CONTENTS

Introduction:

Seven Reasons Why You Need This Book

If you're a new supervisor, or soon to be one, and have never interviewed anyone, this book should help prepare you to do one of your most important jobs.

If you manage people or have hired personnel, then, before you start reading, answer these seven questions.

1. Have you replaced a number of people on the same job during the past year?
2. Have any of the people you replaced been promoted to better-paying, more skilled jobs inside the company?
3. Has anyone gone off to a better-paying, more skilled job in another organization, even though your company offers excellent opportunities?
4. Have you had to discipline an employee in the last year?
5. Have you put an employee on performance probation or given similar warnings within the last two years?
6. Has upper management complained recently of high turnover in personnel?
7. Have you fired someone recently?

If you answered *yes* to question 2 and *no* to all the rest, you may not need this book. Still, reading it might be fun and educational. If you answered *no* to question 2 and *yes* to one of the others, you'll find this book useful. If you answered *yes* to more than two of the questions other than question 2, you NEED this book.

People often complain that "they don't make employees like they used to," but you have no way of knowing if that's because something's wrong with the people you hire or because something's wrong with the way you're hiring them. Unfortunately, most organizations don't train their managers to interview, select, and hire the right people. The smaller the organization, the less likely it is to deliver training in this most sensitive area. And good interviewers are made, not born.

When you're promoted or hired on to supervise a work group, the people you inherit resemble relatives. You're stuck with them regardless of what you think or want until you can disown or divorce them—that is, you make the necessary changes or they move on.

What are you going to do then? Hire more of the same? Hopefully, by the time you've finished reading this book, you won't. You'll save yourself from headaches, sleepless nights, and grief when you hire the right people to do the right jobs.

You'll make rational hiring decisions because you'll design job descriptions that zero in on the qualifications and qualities of the person who can do the job. You'll talk less, ask the right—and legal—questions, and listen to the answers. And you'll have some formats on which to do your preinterview homework.

Chapter 1

You Do the Hiring

That's true, you know. Personnel screens the candidates, but you make the final selection of those people you hire. In fact, the organization relies on you to hire the most profitable personnel for your unit. However, anyone who's ever worked in the personnel industry will tell you that many managers hire for the wrong reasons.

Two Axioms of Personnel

1. People hire on the basis of chemistry.
2. People hire in their own image.

Many people hire employees because they get along well with them. That usually means the candidate seemed to devour the interviewer's every word as he or she dominated the conversation with talk about the organization and war stories about his or her career. Even if the supervisor did question the candidate, the final decision came down to how well they got along during the interview. As one supervisor confessed, "I hired him because he understood what kind of guy I am. How could I know he had so many hangups about working for a large corporation?"

People in the personnel industry will also tell you that employers often ask for people with "that IBM image." Well, they may ask for it, but they frequently turn that image down and hire in their own. People who talk like them, look like them, think like them have a leg up on people more qualified than the IBM types. Instead of hiring the best or most qualified people, they hire their own reflections.

But that usually leads to conflict: "That woman's as stubborn as I am. I can't get her to do anything more than the minimum."

Hiring the wrong people costs the organization too much money. It creates production or service problems and generates ill-will from customers or vendors. It produces interpersonal problems and adds to expensive personnel turnover or other personnel problems. If your organization experiences more than a 25 percent turnover a year, it suffers serious personnel problems.

But, most important, hiring the wrong people costs you mentally, emotionally, and professionally. One supervisor's *wife* complained:

Carl's a wreck. He comes home muttering about Ron every day, dreams nightmares about him.

He's constantly patching things up with other department heads. He spends more time putting out the fires Ron lights than anything else. He's arrogant, pompous, and condescending. He doesn't even do his job well. He thinks he does—and he thinks he does everyone else's jobs better than they do, too. Oh, I wish Carl hadn't hired that man.

When people take on employees who can't do their jobs or can't do them well, they spend too much time training, coaching, counseling, or doing repair work. Keeping up, meeting the unit's objectives, monitoring the work of their other employees produce enough stress as it is. Add a problem employee to that list and the stress can become more than many supervisors can handle. They're trying to do too much with too little.

Their managers notice it, too. They get evaluated on their unit's productivity, and they also get evaluated on the basis of how well they hire and develop their personnel. How does it look if they hire people who not only can't do the work but disrupt the organization? Want to bet that Carl also wishes he hadn't hired "that man"?

(There was a "Carl," but the Carl of this book is a composite of many supervisors and managers trained to interview effectively. So, when I talk about him or what he does, keep in mind that this character functions as a role model made up of many different people just like you.)

When Carl hired Ron, he had Personnel run a blind ad for a detail man for his commercial design drafting department. "Two years experience reading blueprints and producing detail drawings." That's what he gave them to work with. When Personnel asked for more information, he answered, "Hey! That's it. That's what I need."

When Ron showed up, carrying a less than impressive résumé that Carl barely read, the interview went something like this:

4

Carl: You can read blueprints?

Ron: Sure.

Carl: Where you from?

Ron: Peoria.

Carl: You don't say. My wife's from Peoria. We met when I was in the air force, in Edwardsville. She was living in St. Louis then. I just got back from Korea. You ever in the service?

Ron: Yeah. Air force, too.

Carl: Most of the men in the department were in the air force. You should get along just fine. Where'd you go to school?

Ron: City Tech High School.

Carl: That's a pretty good school, I hear. I didn't go to school around here. I grew up back East. I wouldn't be living here if I hadn't met my wife, and her family's here. You know how it is.

Ron: Yeah.

Carl: You married?

Ron: No. Engaged.

Carl: That's good. I like stable and steady men. I really don't like single men that much. Had a forty-year-old bachelor working for me once. We didn't along too well. A pretty good draftsman, but I don't know. We didn't have that much in common. You know what I mean? You can draw, can't you.

Ron: I brought a portfolio. Mind if I put it up on the desk?

Carl: Sure. Go ahead. [*Looking at the drawings*] Pretty good. That house. I worked on one just like that. Never did like the elevation. I like older, more traditional architecture. How about you?

Ron: Yeah. In fact, I'm remodeling a house now. We're going to live in it when we get married. It's nearly a hundred years old.

Carl: No kiddin'. I'd like to see it. Where is it?

Ron: It's down near the bottom, not far from. . . .

And so the story goes. You know the unhappy ending, too. "But jeez, he seemed like such a nice kid."

5

He may have seemed like "a nice kid," and maybe he was in some ways, but he wasn't what Carl needed. Still, because Carl made so many interviewing errors, he had no way of knowing just what kind of employee Ron would be.

He didn't give Personnel enough information. He didn't have an interview plan or guide. He ignored Ron's résumé. He asked all the wrong questions and thought too well of the answers, making too many assumptions. He dominated the conversation, which he kept on a personal level. He answered some of his own questions, and he accepted a man with the wrong kind of experience—in single-family homes rather than commercial buildings. In short, Ron may have been a good employee for a different environment. Carl blew it.

- -

Proactive Hiring

Anticipating possible problems and preventing them
by knowing what you need and want,
and hiring the people who fill the bill.

- -

Carl knows better now. He still hires nice people, but they're nice people with the background and ability to do the job and work within the context of the organization. Now, he's hiring *proactively*.

That means, instead of reacting to the crises produced by bringing in the wrong people, he's anticipating possible problems and preventing them. He's deciding before the interview what he really needs and wants—in terms of experience, skill, education, training, and personal traits—and matching the candidates with the requirements. Hiring proactively takes more time and effort up front than doing hiring on the basis of chemistry or self-image, but the rewards are worth it.

Chapter 2

How to Prepare for the Interview With a Job and Task Analysis

Remember, you're filling a position, not looking for a friend, but even when you look for a friend, you should have some idea of what you want in and of a person. You have some idea of what being a friend consists of. When you interview to fill a position, the same should hold true. You need to know what the job consists of.

Carl's now much more prepared to interview, select, and hire people for his unit. He completed the job analysis shown in Exhibit 1 and converted it into a task analysis (Exhibit 2) that he now uses for designing a job listing and interview guide (Exhibit 3). With these instruments, he knows what his job, skill, and person requirements are, and he knows what questions to ask to make sure he gets the right information for hiring the right person for the job.

Take a look at Exhibit 1. It outlines a position or job, which consists of objectives and tasks or activities. The analysis further shows when tasks are performed, how frequently, and for how many hours a week.

In Carl's analysis of the detailer's job, he identified the most important task for reaching the objective of the job: drafting detailed drawings. It's done daily, five days a week, for an average of five hours a day. Other tasks he found were performed on an "as needed" basis ("Need") or "when possible" ("Poss").

Don't take the details of the sample analysis too literally. The exhibit is designed to illustrate *any* job analysis. Yours may have fewer or more tasks, with

(text continues on page 9)

Exhibit 1. Job analysis.

INSTRUCTIONS: (1) Begin each task name with an action verb; (2) keep task names short; (3) list tasks taking the most time first; (4) #/Hours refers to number of days per week and how much time, in hours, each task takes.

D = Daily   W = Weekly   M = Monthly

Job Title: Drafter—Detailer Department/Unit: Commercial Design
Objectives: To produce final drawings showing dimensions, materials, and other data for use in commercial construction.
Job Qualifications: AAS, required, 4 years exper. preferred; 2 years minimum in comm design.

#	Tasks	D	W	M	Other	#/Hours
1.	Draft detailed draw-					
	ings from rough					
	or general design					
	drawings on					
	computer.	x				5 25
2.	Draw wiring					
	schematics on					

Frequency/Estimated Time spans the D, W, M, Other, #/Hours columns.

#	Tasks	D	W	M	Other	#/Hours	
	computer.	x				2	5
3.	Trace finished						
	drawings to						
	semis for stats						
	on computer.				Need	2	2
4.	Work with design						
	team.				Need	1	4
5.	Work with drafter						
	to learn general						
	drafting duties						
	(OJT).				Poss	1	4

(Column header above the table reads: Frequency/Estimated Time, with sub-columns D | W | M | Other | #/Hours)

different objectives and different frequency and time estimates. In short, Exhibit 1 shows that every job objective describes its contribution to the unit's goals, and the list of tasks explains how the objectives are reached. Your job, before listing a job opening, is to evaluate the position in these terms and then look for the right people to do those things.

The Job Analysis

The objective gives direction to the job analysis as well as to the job, and the list of tasks gives substance to the objective.

An objective in a job analysis consists of what a person in that position has to accomplish. In Carl's case, the target is to produce final drawings showing dimensions, materials, and other data for use in commercial construction. By specifying results and by emphasizing them, objectives give direction to the person doing the job.

That Ron couldn't do his job as a *commercial* design detailer well caused Carl considerable grief. But Carl himself bought the problem, because while Ron may have been an A-number-one, crackerjack single-family residence detailer (and the dialogue intimated as much), the job's objective calls for *commercial* design. Carl wound up looking at the wrong person to do the job.

The job analysis also spells out what a person should bring to the party in order to do the job properly. Again, in our example, a minimum requirement is an Associates degree in architectural science. Ron, as the dialogue shows, went to City Tech High School, but not to college. He didn't have the education he needed to do his job. Therefore, he not only couldn't do his job well, he probably also felt the pressure of being underqualified. Like many people in that situation, the young man may have tried to make up for his lack of education with arrogance.

Finally, the job analysis spells out the tasks that achieve the objective. Only by listing all the primary tasks can a supervisor decide what skills are needed to do the job. Only by knowing what skills are needed can the supervisor find out if a candidate has them.

A job analysis contains no magic that produces Mr. or Ms. Right-for-the-Job, but it does contain one factor that keeps our noses pretty much pointed in the correct direction: action verbs.

Action verbs force us to look for skills, for the ability to *do* things. They even get us to look beyond character traits or personality characteristics to *how* people act in certain circumstances, as when Carl wrote, "work with design team." The person Carl hires has to have the ability to work with people as a team member, rather than push them around. Action verbs remind us why we hire people: to do things and to do them well.

That seems obvious enough, but you'd be amazed how few interviewers ever probe for the candidate's ability to achieve the objectives or at least for his or her ability to learn how to perform the tasks necessary to achieve them. But, then again, you've probably been interviewed often enough to know how sad but true that is.

You can avoid that mistake by starting now to plan your next round of interviews. I've reprinted a blank version of Exhibit 1 at the end of the book. If you don't fill one out for each position for which you have responsibility, then at least fill one out for a position you know you have to fill in the near future. Complete the assignment before continuing on to the next section.

The Task Analysis

"What has to be done" is the task, the duty, the responsibility. By separating the "tasks" from the objectives, you identify exactly what a person in this position has to do to accomplish the contribution he or she's supposed to make to your unit and to the organization.

Take a look at Exhibit 2 before going on. It's the task analysis Carl completed. When you come back to the text, I'll go over why I put it together and what you can accomplish by using it.

In a job analysis, you strip out the means and conditions from the objectives of the job. By doing a task analysis, on the other hand, you describe the regular and usual *activities* that make up the means

(text continues on page 15)

Exhibit 2. Task analysis.

INSTRUCTIONS: (1) List one task name at a time in order of importance; (2) list skills needed for doing each task in order of importance.

E = Essential **I** = Important **N** = Nice to have

Job Title: Drafter-Detailer

Department/Unit: Commmercial Design

	Tasks/Skills	Importance
1.	Draft detailed drawings from	
	rough or general design	
	drawings on computer:	
	a. Operate Macintosh.	
	b. Operate laser printer.	E
	c. Use a variety of drafting	
	software.	E
	d. Read blueprints.	E
	e. Detail structural designs	
	of commercial buildings.	E
	f. Draw plumbing schematics	

	Tasks/Skills	Importance
	on the computer.	E
	g. Read code manuals.	E
	h. Read spec sheets.	E
	i. Do algebra on a computer.	E
	j. Manually draw anything	
	done on the computer.	I
2.	Draw wiring schematics on	
	the computer:	
	a. Read code manuals.	E
	b. Read electrical spec sheets.	E
	c. Draw electrical schematics	
	on the computer.	E
3.	Trace finished drawings to semis	
	for stats on computer:	

Exhibit 2 *(continued)*.

	Tasks/Skills	Importance
	a. Operate laser printer.	E
	b. Trace manually.	I
4.	Attend design meetings:	
	a. Take notes of discussions.	E
	b. Discuss structural details with architects.	I
	c. Draw rough details during discussion.	N
5.	Work with drafter to learn general drafting duties:	
	a. Place buildings on location.	N
	b. Arrange office and retail layouts.	N
	c. Draw elevations with	

	Tasks/Skills	Importance
	paints and washes.	N
	d. Landscape.	N
6.	Other skills.	

and conditions of the job. That list of activities describes how the job gets done: Operate the Macintosh equipment, use a variety of drafting software, and so on. Carl now knows he should find out whether the candidate can do any of those things, before checking to see if he or she's married (a highly suspect question to begin with).

Besides listing the specifics of daily activities, the

task analysis does something that may be even more essential: uncover the skills a person has to have, which the job analysis merely implies, such as computer operation, manual drawing, technical reading, and communication. All those skills are identified in the tasks listed. Designing ways to test those skills should play a large role in Carl's planning for his next round of interviews.

The list also helps you decide the kind of person you need in the job you're analyzing. Job skills form only one part of the requirements. In Carl's case, teamwork's required—initiative, creativity, communication. The person Carl needs has to fit in with a group, that's true, but having been in the air force doesn't have much to do with it.

The task analysis also leads you to decide on the *most important* skills by separating the essential from the important and the nice-to-have skills. The analysis helps you establish your priorities, the priorities on which you'll focus during an interview. In fact, the analysis provides you with your "knockout" questions. If a candidate lacks many or most of the *essential* skills needed, you simply knock him or her out of the running.

Between the job analysis and the task analysis, you have a solid job description. You can use these tools not only for designing a job listing and interview guide but also for designing a work measurement or management system (a topic for another book).

Take out some time now for doing a task analysis of the job analysis you did previously (a blank task analysis is in the Appendix). When you're finished, go on to the next section.

The Job Listing

Carl really blundered when he failed to give Personnel an adequate description of the job he was trying to fill. The wrong information came into the interview because not enough information was circulated to the public. A sufficient description helps people screen themselves out as much as it helps other people screen themselves in. The self-screening process then helps Personnel prescreen the more viable candidates for you.

I don't include a job listing format here because most personnel departments have their own preferred form. However, you can build one for yourself if your organization doesn't have one just by designing it around these requirements for a job listing.

- It must have a job title.
- It must state the primary objective of the job, not necessarily all objectives.
- It must state job qualifications, both those you require and those you prefer.
- It must list the most important tasks in the task analysis.

When Personnel writes the ad or posts the listing on a job posting board, it may not include all the tasks in your analysis, but that's one of the reasons why you identify the most important ones first. That way, it has some idea of what you need the most. Then it will add other appropriate information, e.g., "competitive salary" and "good benefits."

The personnel department will screen the responses for you, but you must be ready to take up the chore from there. That's why you design an interview guide.

Chapter 3

How to Use Your Interview Guide for Making Sound Hiring Decisions

Carl prided himself on his spontaneity during an interview. You saw what it got him.

You don't want to *eliminate* spontaneity, but shouldn't rely on it either. As in any other management activity, effective interviewing depends on a sound plan: an interview guide and the tools for digging out the information needed for making a rational choice.

Exhibit 3 illustrates portions of an interview guide. It's abbreviated or truncated, but it will give you a model for designing your own. Read through it before going on. That way you'll be familiar with everything referred to in the following section.

On a T-chart, so named for the grid's T shape, build an interview guide out of the job and task analyses. Label each side of the line across the top with categories of items you'll list.

On the left side of the T-chart, list the job's objectives, qualifications, tasks or activities, skills, and personal characteristics. The job qualifications, as you can see, refer to educational and experience requirements. The duties and functions consist of the tasks or activities involved in the job. All these factors are what we call the position specifications.

On the other side of the T-chart, list the experience, the skills, education and training, and/or personal characteristics needed for doing the tasks, meeting the obligations, and fulfilling the objectives of the job. But list them in a unique way. Instead of writing comments, ask questions.

The organization of the questions is as important as the questions themselves. Three categories organize the skills analysis, and when taken in the order of their importance they will help you conduct the proper interview for each applicant. They are (1) previous work experience (2) education and training, and (3) personal characteristics.

Put *all* your essential questions in writing. Leaving nothing to chance, except *the questions that the résumé or application triggers or that occur to you while the candidate is speaking.* You see, I haven't eliminated spontaneity, I have just put it into its proper place.

Work Experience

A best possible choice will have work experience. In some cases, especially if you're looking for a trainee,

(text continues on page 22)

Exhibit 3. Job listing and interview guide.

INSTRUCTIONS: (1) Using your job and task analyses, complete each category on the left-hand side of the T-chart; (2) on the right-hand side, list questions to ask. Use extra pages if you need them.

Position Specifications	*Interview Guide*

Job Title

Drafter—Detailer

Objectives

To produce final drawings showing dimensions, materials, and other data for use in construction.

Job qualifications

AAS, required
4 years experience preferred, 2 years minimum in commercial design.

Duties and Functions

Draft detailed drawings from rough or general design drawings on computer.
Draw wiring schematics on the computer.
Trace finished drawings to semis for stats on computer.
Attend design meetings.

Work Experience

What were your duties in your most recent position?
What did you like most about your work? Least? Why?
What kind of work have you done on the Macintosh/Laser Printer?
Describe your most difficult assignment and what made it so hard?
Tell me about your most personally rewarding work and what made it rewarding for you?
Under what conditions do you feel most comfortable working? That is, under close supervision, or little supervision, with a team or by yourself?
Tell me about your working relation-

(continued)

Exhibit 3 *(continued).*

Position Specifications	*Interview Guide*

Work with drafter to learn general drafting duties.

ships with the professional staff and other people.

Skills

Skill Requirements

Operate Macintosh.
Operate laser printer.
Use a variety of drafting software.
Read blueprints, code manuals and structural and electrical spec sheets.
Detail structural designs of commercial buildings.
Draw plumbing schematics on the computer.
Do algebra on a computer.
Manually draw anything done on the computer.
Draw electrical schematics on the computer.
Trace manually.
Take notes of discussions.
Discuss structural details with architects and draw rough de-

Describe the software you've used either on the job or in school.
Here's a blueprint. Please read it and explain at least one structural problem you think you see.
Here's a wiring diagram of a retail space. Locate the connections for cash registers and rough out the schematic.

Education/Training

At school, what were your best subjects? Your worst?
In all your education, what subjects did you like the most? The least? Why?

Person Characteristics

I'd like to know about your experiences working on a team.

tails during discussion.

Person Qualifications

Work well in a team.
Communicate well, especially with drafters and sub-contractors.
Solve problems.
Handle more than one task at a time.
Accept change well.
Accept direction and supervision well.
Start quickly and apply self to the job.
Pay attention to detail.
Willing to accept extra duties as they arise.
Want to grow with a growing firm.

When you're confronted with making a decision and you have no clear-cut options, how do you go about solving the problem? What steps do you take?
What's your best time of day for being the most productive?
Where in your family do you fall? Youngest? Oldest? Middle?
What kind of responsibilities did your family expect of you as you were growing up?
When someone gives you an order, how do you feel?
The job description of this position ends with "and perform duties as they are assigned." What do you think of that?
Though a career plan isn't a requirement of the job, what do you see yourself doing five years from now?

a specific kind of work experience isn't as important as work experience period. You want to know if the person knows what work is and if he or she did well at whatever he or she did. The skills the candidate learned in, say, part-time summer jobs while going to school may transfer. At least they tell you that he or she is trainable.

In the situation in our story, Carl needs work experience that translates directly to the job he's advertising. He can't use a trainee. That's why he looks first at a person's work experience. He wants to see if the applicant can do the job, and past history *may* indicate that he or she can do it and do it well.

I say "may indicate" because the axiom in the sidebar is true in many but not all cases. Many factors independent of the candidate's skill and energy can contribute to a good or a poor performance on another job. For example, the candidate may have worked for someone with a particular knack for drawing out the best from this person. Carl may not be as skilled. Or, the person may have received assignments beyond his or her capability, so he or she always looked bad. Carl can assign work appropriate to the candidate's capability and he or she will do well.

Carl needs to ask the right questions about *what* the person *did* in previous positions so he can decide whether the person has the specific or transferable skills needed to do the job. No one can determine how well-qualified a candidate is unless the applicant's skills can be tested either orally or in some physical way. That's why some organizations use assessment center techniques to evaluate the capabilities of their job candidates.

An assessment center requires a candidate to perform tasks that simulate those he or she would have to

Another Axiom

Past performance is the best indicator
of future performance.

do on the job. Some people use real situations taken
from the position's daily experience. A group of experts
or people specifically trained to judge performance
observe the candidate in action and evaluate the performance. A good performer then goes on to additional
interviews; a poor performer receives a polite thank-
you-for-interviewing letter.

Returnees

Let's not forget the large body of women now entering
the work force after raising their families. Many of them
may not have the specific work experience you're
looking for, but unless you absolutely have to have
certain skills, you shouldn't overlook whatever transferable skills they have, especially if they have helped in
a family business, assisted a salesman husband, or
have had similar experiences.

Also consider the details of volunteer work, but more
important, don't turn up your nose at the role a woman
has played in the home. Few managers in business
and industry can match the organizational budgeting,
and communicating skills of a housewife shepherding
husband and children.

Work History

Nothing contributes more to a candidate's value than
his or her experience doing the work you need done or
experience that easily transfers. So focus on that as-
pect first. If you don't see what you need in a candidate's résumé, unless you have an extremely good
reason for doing so, don't call this person in for an
interview. If you do call such a person in, look for a

substantive backup to the claims of the résumé within the first ten minutes of the interview or don't bother going on. "Thank you, and we'll let you know," is all you need to say.

Education and Training

Educational background is a good beginning only. Not that this background doesn't matter, it's just that work experience is much more important. In some ways, the distinction has to do with the difference between *knowing what something is or knowing how to do something* and *actually doing it.* I can tell you how to get to China, but I've never been there. And if you ask me to fly the plane, I promise you we will not get there alive, even though I know how, in principle, to make an airplane go.

Again, if you're looking for a trainee, then a fresh grad just out of high school or college, with little or no work experience, may be just what you need. Go for it, but consider also that even with an appropriate *formal* education, a trainee's profitability may not show up for a period anywhere from six months to two years (depending upon the degree of sophistication or complexity of the job).

When planning questions about educational history, distinguish between formal education and skill training. Formal education focuses on knowledge and understanding, not doing. Since you need a doer, balance book-larnin' against other forms of larnin'. Work experience, again, even if it's not in the kind of job you're trying to fill, has given the candidate training in work habits, organization, time management, and other worthwhile work skills.

On the other hand, formal education also has given the applicant skills in addition to knowledge of pure subject matter. If, for example, you work for a market research firm, a candidate with a degree in marketing would be of greater interest to you than one with a degree in medieval literature. At the same time, both of them have learned how to research a problem, how to look at a situation from a variety of directions, and how to organize and present information. If you're looking for someone to groom for management, the literature student may not be such a bad choice (if you're willing to train him or her).

In fact, studies have shown that liberal arts majors take a little longer and require a few more resources to train in various technical fields, but they go into management more frequently and at a faster pace than do people who are more technically trained. They also prove to be more effective managers than many MBAs.

So when you prepare an interview guide, devise questions that probe what the applicant studied, what he or she did or didn't like about his or her studies, in what the candidate did or didn't do well—and why. Real aptitudes or deficiencies show up in the answers to "why."

Also consider how well a person did in subjects he or she *didn't* like but had to study. An A in that class may indicate a facet of character as well as intelligence.

A Grade Point Average (GPA) of B from a person who worked full-time while going through school might be worth more than a straight-A average from someone whose parents paid all the bills. The working student not only did well in his or her studies but juggled two full-time jobs in the process. That kind of organizational skill and concentration will prove worthwhile on the job, to be sure.

At the same time, overall GPA isn't as important as the GPA in the major field of study, especially if the field prepares the candidate to do the job. An A in basket-weaving 101 gets added into the overall tally, but you don't need that.

Academics is only one side of a person's school experience. Skill training of any kind, leadership training, and leadership roles in school also contribute to a person's preparedness to do the job you're hiring for. *Not* working one's way through school is not altogether that bad (especially if the grades were good) as long as the student also has had some genuine growth experiences: extracurricular activities, active roles played on the campus, responsible positions assumed, and other features of school life that contribute to rounding out a person's abilities and character.

Subject matter learned or skills acquired aside, a person's education or training demonstrates that the candidate is *trainable*. Sometimes, again especially when looking for a trainee, if the specific skills needed aren't there but a candidate has all the other characteristics you need or want, you should consider the possibilities. After weighing the cost of training against the benefits of hiring an inexperienced person, you may decide to go ahead and take the chance.

Although education or training is important, the less recent a person's education, the smaller the role it should play in the hiring decision. Check on what the candidate has studied since leaving school.

Someone who has quit studying after being graduated from high school or college has quit growing. Training and education should be an ongoing process. Beware, particularly, the candidate who boasts of ancient school history in answer to the question, "What do you consider to be your finest accomplishment?"

Yet nothing is more disappointing or frustrating than hiring the well-trained or educated specialist you need only to find out, as Carl did, that you hired the wrong person for the organization. A skilled, educated candidate could turn out to be absolutely wrong for the job if his or her personal history doesn't fit. That's why you look at the person characteristics next.

Person Characteristics

You hire a skilled person, not just skills. Ignore the person and you're likely to find yourself with the proverbial fish out of water thrashing about until he or she finds where he or she fits or gets out. Carl was (too) interested in the person and not the skills, but he was interested in the wrong aspects of the person. On the other hand, some supervisors don't want to investigate an applicant's personal characteristics at all—too private, too psychological. Yet, success or failure could hinge on one character trait.

If the truism in the sidebar is accurate, then you need to know a whole lot about a candidate before you decide whether to hire him or her. Inquiries about what he or she's like as a person constitute a major part of the following guide. Here's a list of sample questions, some of which you might find a bit too personal for your liking, but they mean a great deal to a successful interview.

Personal Habits

1. What's your best time of day, the time you feel most productive?
2. What happens to your energy level after lunch? If it slacks off, what do you do to recharge?
3. What do you consider to be your most admirable habit, the thing you do regularly and almost unconsciously?
4. What do you think is your least admirable habit, the thing you do that other people say irritates them or that you personally wish you didn't do?
5. Of all the things you do, which do you enjoy the most and what makes them enjoyable?
6. Of all the things you do, which do you enjoy the least? What makes them bad for you, and why do you do them?

Social Relationships

1. When you're talking with someone, how do you make sure you understand what the other person's talking about?
2. When someone needs help with something important to him or her but that can interfere with your work, what do you do?

27

3. If a group of coworkers invite you to go out for a drink or a bite to eat after work and you have no other plans, what do you do?
4. Which would you rather do, watch a ball game or play in one?
5. If someone else's work were backing up while you were handling yours well and on time, what would you do?
6. During a break, which would you prefer to do: Read a book or engage in small talk?
7. If someone in the group whom you liked was making a lot of errors and causing problems for other people but didn't realize it, how would you handle it?

Leadership

1. While your supervisor is on vacation, in spite of the explicit instructions left behind, the unit's productivity is faltering and upper management's upset about it. What do you do?
2. Rumors about a possible cutback in personnel in your unit have been circulating for a few days and have finally reached you. How do you deal with them?
3. You're serving on a committee and a problem arises that the group can't solve. Suddenly it occurs to you that important information is missing. Which do you do: Suggest that someone research the needed data or volunteer to do the job yourself?
4. A department on which yours depends for information often fails to send the information on to you. You know the supervisor there better than your supervisor does. How do you handle the situation?
5. You and several other employees think that your supervisor has made a mistake or is wrong in the way he or she is handling the people in the unit. Which do you do: Nothing, join together with the others to talk it over with your supervisor, or talk to the supervisor on your own?

6. If management asks you to head up a task force to solve a quality control problem, what would you do: turn it down, accept it reluctantly, or accept it enthusiastically?
7. Your supervisor wrongly accuses a coworker of doing something and your coworker seems too passive to respond. What do you do?

Family Background

1. What is your position in your family? Are you an only child, the oldest, youngest, or in the middle?
2. What responsibilities did your family expect you to assume as you were growing up?
3. If you had a sibling, how did you feel when he or she alone got special attention from a parent? How did you handle it?
4. Which parent disciplined you the most, and how did you feel about being disciplined?
5. How did you feel about the rules your parents made you obey?
6. How do you handle family conflicts?
7. When a family conflict involves you, what responsibility do you assume for creating it, and what responsibility do you assume for resolving it?

Those questions are obviously not exhaustive; they only indicate the possibilities. But their answers tell you about how the candidate works, how the person interacts with other people, and how he or she accommodates to a group. Ask what you think is important to ask, as long as the questions conform to rules set down by the Equal Employment Opportunity Commission (EEOC) based on the Civil Rights Act of 1964 and other pieces of civil rights legislation. Whether you *want* to ask some of those questions, even if they are allowed, is a matter of choice.

Permissible and Impermissible Questions

Questions related to the candidate's family background are permissible if they

- Are clearly job related
- Are asked of every candidate
- Don't have an adverse impact on any specific group of persons

Any questions are permissible as long as they are bona fide—*as long as they meet the criteria just listed.* So, what can't you ask?

Unless the questions pertain to bona fide occupational qualifications (or BFOQs), you are forbidden by law to make any distinctions related to:

Age	Race
Disabilities	Creed
Ethnicity	National origin
Religion	Child care
Arrest records	arrangements
Transportation	Spouse's feelings
General health	about travel away
Group affiliations	from home
Sex	Political beliefs

Those are the main points. If your application form or interview guide isn't already devoid of all those issues, it should be. Several pieces of federal and state or local legislation protect people from discrimination based on those protected factors: The Civil Rights Act of 1964, Age Discrimination in Employment Act, The Rehabilitation Act, and parallel state and local laws.

In Conclusion

An interview guide provides you with a rational plan for investigating a person's background with respect to work history, education and training, and personal characteristics. Type a permanent copy of the guide, leaving space in each category on the right side so that you can add questions based on the résumés or applications you'll be seeing. That way, each time you have to interview another candidate, you need only pull out your standard, preprinted, ready-to-use form.

Chapter 4

Using a Résumé as a Basis for Forming Probing Questions

I am assuming that a personnel department pre-screens your candidates. Someone else makes the decision about whether these people meet the basic requirements in the job listing. Personnel sends you selected paperwork to review before calling the candidates in to interview. That doesn't happen everywhere, and where you work, you could be the person to whom a résumé is sent directly. Whichever's the case, with a résumé in hand, you're ready to decide whether a certain candidate's among the best possible choices.

You've probably noticed some questions made conspicuous by their absence from the interview guide. The applicant's documents should answer some questions I didn't ask. For example, you could have asked, "Where did you go to school," but in all likelihood the application or the résumé answered that question. The same is probably true for questions about current or past employers.

Instead of asking obvious questions, you can use the candidate's materials to form collateral questions, such as "What did you study at Tech College?" or "What were your primary responsibilities at Adams, Baker, and Charles Architects?" What an applicant did at school or at work is the interesting and important information.

Reading a résumé includes more than looking over the person's job history and education. It helps you make decisions or ask questions. For example:

Some Useful Tips About Reading a Résumé

- Use data on a résumé to plan specific questions about the person's qualifications or background.
- Prescreened or not, read printed matter anyway; what Personnel knows, you need to know too.
- Read materials *before* the candidate comes into the room; it makes a person uncomfortable to watch you read about him or her in his or her presence.
- A résumé is advertising; take it with a grain of salt.
- Look for a gap in the history; it could indicate a red flag or a positive, personal growth experience; check it out.
- Check out military experience; skill or leadership training and experience may lurk there.
- Don't pass over avocations; skills and experience hide there, too.

- The information in the résumé helps you decide whether you want to see the person it describes. How closely does the résumé track with the needs in the position specifications? Does the candidate identify the proper work experience, education, and person characteristics?
- Keeping in mind that a résumé is a piece of advertising (sometimes a lot of hype), reading it helps you form possible knockout questions: "What did you do during this gap between graduation and your first position?" "Describe your work with a laser printer." "What experience do you have with wiring diagrams in high-rise office buildings?"
- It helps you form questions that determine whether you want to see the candidate a second time.

A sample résumé, with some pertinent questions, is shown in Exhibit 4. Read it before continuing.

Exhibit 4. Using the résumé to formulate interview questions.

Possible Questions	Résumé
	GEORGIA SMITH
	PROFESSIONAL OBJECTIVE
What plans do you have for more training?	Seeking a position in a high caliber architectural firm, particularly one specializing in commercial structures, that will enable me to use my experience and education in this field, gain additional on-the-job experience, and meet the qualifications for a drafter's position.
	EDUCATION
What courses? Best? Worst? Favorite? Least liked? GPA?	**Ferguson Technical College,** Ferguson, Missouri August 1980 to June 1982 Associate in Architectural Science Major: Drafting Minor: Art
	PROFESSIONAL EXPERIENCE
Why did go with him and now want to leave? Why the gap in time?	**Bernard Adams Associates,** St. Charles, Missouri July 1984 to the present Drafter—detailer **Adams, Baker, and Charles Architects,** Kirkwood, Missouri

(continued)

---

*Adapted from a model résumé in Bobbi Linkemer, *How to Write an Effective Résumé* (New York: AMACOM, 1987), another title in the Successful Office Skills Series.

Exhibit 4 *(continued).*

Possible Questions	*Résumé*
What were you doing between graduation and 10/83?	October 1983 to May 1984 Drafter—detailer

PERSONAL AND PROFESSIONAL ASSETS

Portfolio?

As a professional in commercial building drafting, I draw well manually and paint as well as work with a variety of software (MS-DOS, Apple). I relate well to architects and coworkers, and have worked directly with the clients' engineers at times. I learn new systems easily and rapidly; take direction well and have experience in a wide variety of commercial design projects (including high-rise office buildings and garden office parks). I am dependable, enthusiastic, conscientious, eager to learn, honest and committed to my employer.

What kinds of experiences with architects, engineers?

AFFILIATIONS AND ACTIVITIES

American Association of Architects and Drafters—local chapter.

When on active duty?

Navy Active Reserve—Seaman First Class.

PERSONAL DATA

Birthdate:	July 15, 1960
Health:	Excellent
References:	Available upon request
Flexibility:	Willing to travel or relocate

Chapter 5

The Four Stages of the Initial Interview and How to Conduct Them

Some people say that the first interview should take at least four hours. I say, two ought to do the job.

In fact, if you plan it right, the interview could take as little as ten minutes—just long enough to find out if it's worthwhile to give this candidate the full time. The answers to the knockout questions you've devised after reading the application or résumé should tell you if he or she can do or learn to do the job. If neither seems likely, give the person a ten-minute courtesy interview and send him or her packing.

If it seems that the applicant is a pretty good possibility, give him or her as much time as you need to work through the interview guide—up to the point where he or she either is knocked out or passes muster. The interview should progress through four stages: (1) openers, (2) the inquiry, (3) the exchange, and (4) the close.

The openers include greetings, businesslike small talk, and putting the candidate at ease. *The inquiry* consists of reviewing the person's work history, educational background, and personal characteristics. *The exchange* is the time at which you satisfy his or her curiosity about the job, the organization, the salary range, and the benefits. *The close* consists of confirming the candidate's interest and expressing yours before deciding on the next step. Each stage has its own objective and trial close.

I'll not only discuss each stage separately, I'll also

illustrate each with a brief dialogue so you can get the flavor.

Openers

You set the stage for the interview, the objective of this stage, by the manner in which you greet the candidate: a warm and sincere smile, a firm handshake, a pleasant, businesslike conversation that ends by explaining the interview's purpose, and how you will conduct it.

Carl: Hello. I'm Carl Schneider. After only talking on the phone, I'm pleased to meet you in person.

Georgia: Thank you. It's good to meet you, too.

Carl: When we talked, you seemed to have a serious interest in a career in architecture.

Georgia: Yes. My father's an architect. I'd like to be one, too, some day, but I don't think I'm ready for it yet. I should take it in stages, I think.

Carl: That's interesting.

Georgia: I have the drawing ability, but I'm not sure I'm as creative now as I will be after I've been around the business for awhile.

Carl: You seem to have a plan in mind. Not too many people, even my age, have that good a picture of how to get where they want to go. [*After a very brief pause*] Georgia— you mind me using your first name?

Georgia: Not at all.

Carl: Call me Carl. Well, Georgia, the point of this interview is to see if we really are made for each other. I'll want to know things about your experience, your studies, and you. I'll tell you about the job, the company, and benefits. Then, we'll decide where to go from here. You ready for all that?

Georgia: Sure. I'm very interested in the job, as you know.

The Inquiry

Carl learned enough from his openers to want to go on. He also had Georgia talking about herself. That set the stage for the inquiry portion of the interview, the objective of which is to get *as much information about the candidate as you can.*

Remember, you're going to hire someone not only to do a job but also to live with you and other people for at least eight hours a day and at least five days a week. You'll probably have more contact time with this person than you will with your family, so be sure to pick a winner.

You can't do that unless you control the interview. Whoever controls it controls the decision. Since it's your decision to make, you have to prevent the applicant from wresting control from you during the inquiry stage. And, don't think some won't try—especially if they've been sent by a head hunter or personnel consultant. They've been prepped to do just that.

Beware the *prepped* applicant. Take a careful look at anyone who's *been* prepared for the interview. Prepped applicants have been coached on what to say, what to expect, and how to handle themselves in the clinches. They know little more about your organization than what they've been told—usually information you supplied to the coach.

Prepared applicants may have done some homework on their own—for example, they may have consulted Moody's *Industrials* or some other business reference. They know what the organization does and are aware of its gross revenue for the last two years and other financial statement data. If nothing else, they've talked about your organization with a variety of people, some of whom are knowledgeable. But most applicants coming through an agency are prepped, not prepared.

Of the three possibilities for getting into the interview after you've exchanged pleasantries, the first two play right into the hands of the well-prepped applicant. Here are some examples.

The 20 Percent Rule

Talk no more than 20 percent of the time.

Opening the Floodgate:

Carl: Well, Georgia, what questions do you have about the job or the organization?

Digging your Own Grave:

Carl: Well, Georgia, let me tell you about the job and something about the company. Then you can tell me what you think you can do for us.

Well-prepped applicants will want to get as much information about the position as they can. That way they can answer your questions, and make their background fit to a "tee." How can you turn down someone who tells you everything you want to hear?

That's why you also don't start the interview by describing the job in detail, the problems the person might encounter, and the needs the organization has to meet. Instead, you start by asking the other person what he or she knows about the job to see just how well *prepared* he or she is.

Taking Firm Control:

Carl: Well, Georgia, what do you know about the position you're applying for and our organization?

A *prepped* applicant has only as much information as you or the Personnel Department gave to the agency. A *prepared* candidate has that information plus information he or she could have acquired only by doing some research. That extra initiative gives you the right signal. At the same time, as you give the applicant a chance to show off, you also reinforce the behavior you initiated in the openers. The applicant does the talking.

You control the inquiry by asking the right questions and by asking them in the right way. In fact, that's why this stage is called inquiry: It's an investigation into the person's qualifications for doing this job and for belonging to your organization.

Your most important tools during the inquiry are your open-ended questions. These are questions that can't be answered by yes or no. Instead, these questions begin with "who," "why," "where," "when," "what," and "how" to elicit information.

The inquiry may degenerate into an inquisition unless you mix open-end questions with other kinds of "gatekeepers" (such as "Hmm," "I see"), or "open-ended comments," or "pregnant silences," or "feedback" (mirroring or informational and behavioral feedback). We call these communication devises gatekeepers because you use them to start or stop a conversation or some part of it (opening and shutting a gate). All of them open a gate, but informational feedback, as a summary, can shut it as well, ending a conversation or making a transition to another topic.

Gatekeepers in Addition to Open-Ended Questions

- *Open-ended comments:* "Tell me more." "That's interesting." "Go on."
- *Pregnant silence:* A deliberate pause, waiting for the other person to speak or respond to you.
- *Mirroring:* Letting the other person know that you are aware of his or her feelings and are acknowledging them. "You seem angry about something."
- *Informational feedback:* Letting the other person know you understand what he or she said. "Let's see if I have this right. I think you said. . . ."
- *Behavioral feedback:* Letting the other person know how something he or she did or said affects you. "When you said that, I became concerned that you may not be able to do this part of the job."

An overuse of open-ended questions and other gate-keepers may lead to a rambling, unfocused interview in which you keep the candidate talking but not necessarily about what you want to talk about. You must keep the conversation on your chosen track by making "close-ended comments" or by asking "closed-ended questions" and "either/or questions" and by using "laundry lists."

- *Closed-ended comment:* A way to acknowledge what the other person said or to end a conversation or some part of it; "So, you'll do that for me."
- *Closed-ended question:* Questions that have to be answered by "yes," "no," "maybe," or "I don't know." They usually start with a form of the verb "to be," or with "can you," "will you," "do you," "have you"; sometimes they start with an open-ended "W" word, but in a very restrictive context, e.g., "What's in your hand" or "For whom did you say you worked?"
- *Either/or question:* A special class of closed-ended questions (also called forced-choice questions) that helps you sort out an applicant's work-related values, attitudes, and preferences. They're particularly useful when looking into an applicant's personal characteristics. "If you have a choice, would you prefer to work with a team or by yourself?"
- *Laundry list:* A multiple-choice question, but not a forced choice. When the candidate seems confused or appears not to understand a question, you list a series of options.

Look at this little dialogue.

Carl: How would you describe your ideal situation?

Georgia: [*After a pause*] Uh, I don't think I understand the question.

Carl: Your ideal situation—a full-time job, going to school at night? A part-time job, going to school during the day? On-the-job training with a mentor? That's all I'm really looking for.

That's a laundry list. It helps the other person zero in on specific information you want or need.

One type of closed-ended question poisons an interview: the leading question, which you must avoid at all costs. A leading question contains its own answer: "You can operate an Apple, can't you?" The candidate will tell you what you want to hear, which may not be true or accurate.

Anything with a closed-end shares this virtue: It gets at specific facts or confirms opinions. It also brings specific parts of a conversation or the whole conversation to a close: "You think you really want this job?"

That question is another special breed of closed-ended question, a "closer." You wouldn't use the example just given until the end of the interview, but all along the way, you'll want to ask similar questions, called trial closers: "What do you think of what I've said so far?" "Do you see yourself doing that?" This way you can find out if the applicant is interested up to this point. If the person seems hesitant or reluctant, you can find out why by asking for a "process check."

Process checks interrupt the conversation's flow to see if you and the other person are together: "You seem reluctant about what I just asked. I'd like you to share your thoughts with me." "You seem distracted by something. What's happening?" It's poor policy to proceed if the person seems reluctant, disinterested or uninterested, or distracted.

Strange as it may seem, the more the other person talks, the more in control you are. Questioning the other person helps control the conversation by focusing on your agenda. If you talk, you can't find out what you need to know. When the candidate responds to your questions, he or she is doing all the talking and can't force you into his or her agenda.

While the other person talks, you listen, talking only to direct the conversation with questions for clarification, i.e., gatekeepers and feedback. Don't even take notes. Concentrate on what is being said. Watch gestures or body language. You can write a summary of the meeting immediately afterwards.

Taking nonverbals (gestures, body language, facial expressions) and quasiverbals (inflections, tone of voice) too seriously can create misunderstandings because they're vague and ambiguous—open to a wide variety of interpretations even by "the experts." Still, some gestures or body language speak clearly.

Shifting eyes, a lack of focus, an inability to hold your eyes may indicate that the person you are interviewing has difficulty relating to other people, or possibly he or she has something to hide. Whichever interpretation is correct, any of these signals is a negative. If the position calls for a lot of social interaction or trust, they indicate that this person wouldn't mix well.

Stammering, incoherence, or frequent clearing of the throat indicate a lack of self-confidence, an unsureness. If you need someone with drive, self-esteem, and enthusiasm, this one might not be for you.

On the other side of the coin, a person who holds eye contact comfortably (not riveting you with a stare), who speaks fluently and seems at ease too, should be worth pursuing, at least for now.

Before leaving this discussion of the inquiry, let's take a look at a short dialogue that illustrates all the points made. We'll include references to the tools Carl uses by putting terms in brackets.

Carl: You said in your résumé that you're looking for on-the-job experience to help you advance your career. What plans do you have for additional training? [*Open-ended question*]

Georgia: I think I'll stay out of school for a little while longer—maybe a night class or two, but I really need the hands-on work experience.

Carl: Then, you think you've had enough training at Ferguson Technical College. [*Closed-ended comment*]

Georgia:	For now.
Carl:	How about at Adams and Associates? [*Open-ended question*]
Georgia:	What do you mean?
Carl:	Training through experience. Did you get to draw on the computer, use the laser printer, manually draw—things like that? [*Laundry list*]
Georgia:	Well, no. Adams is a very small firm. Most of the work was hand-drawn. But I did have time on the computer at Adams, Baker, and Charles.
Carl:	Which did you prefer—manual drawing or computer drawing? [*Either/or question*]
Georgia:	I enjoy them both, really, but if I have my choice, I like computer drafting, but not elevations. I prefer to do them in water color.
Carl:	Tell me more about the computer drafting. [*Open-ended comment*]

As you can well imagine, this dialogue could continue for many more pages, especially if I included all the *follow-up* questions Carl could ask. A "follow-up question" is one that you ask after the other person answers a question. Here's a place where spontaneity comes into play. Most frequently, a follow-up question will occur to you as a result of the answer to the previous question. The either/or question in the previous dialogue illustrates a common kind of follow-up question.

I hope you get the idea of how to use a mix of questions and comments for getting the applicant to talk to you about him- or herself. In a real conversation, Georgia would probably talk at even greater length in answer to Carl's questions.

There's no set time by which you should bring the inquiry phase to a close. When you think it's time, it's time. Usually, that's when you think all your questions have been answered. Then it's time to move on to the exchange.

The Exchange

I call this stage the exchange because its objective is to give back information in return for the information you've received. That's fair enough, isn't it?

Start the exchange by having the candidate ask you questions. Questions reveal the person's interests, values, attitudes, and concerns. They will fall into two categories: job-oriented questions and self-oriented questions.

1. *Job-oriented questions*—showcasing an interest in the details of the work: the kind of work the candidate would do, where it would be done, and with whom. They refer to opportunities to learn and to grow. The greater the number of these questions, the more likely it is that the candidate is goal-directed and eager-to-work.
2. *Self-oriented questions*—concerning income, benefits, vacations, or social relationships in the office. Expect these questions in a reasonable mix with job-oriented questions, but if the applicant concentrates on these questions, consider carefully whether this person will be the kind of *worker* you want.

Observe how the candidate listens and responds to your answers. A shrug, nonchalance, little or no follow-up, interruptions, disregard for what you're saying—these are negatives. Paying attention, using gatekeepers to keep you talking, smiling with interest, good follow-up questions—these are the signals of someone you might consider further.

Use the exchange to learn more about the candidate as you're giving him or her a chance to learn more about the job, the organization, and you. Remember, you have to live all day, every day on the job with this person.

As you answer questions, make sure you describe the job, the work unit, the company, and the company's benefits; and use trial closes every chance you get. No sense wasting your time if the person's not interested.

The trial close serves a second function. If you have a real interest in this person and he or she doesn't seem too enthusiastic about the job, the organization, or you, a trial close gives you a chance to find out what's missing.

The phrase "trial close" comes from sales, and that's what the two of you are both doing. The candidate's selling his or her skills to you and you're selling the job, the organization, and *yourself* to the candidate.

Since you're both in a selling mode at this stage of the game, you may not want to discuss salary except in noncommittal or general terms—a salary *range* rather than a specific figure. Save that for the hiring interview because then the candidate is in a *selling* mode and *you're* in a *buying* mode. You don't want to lock yourself into a figure until you're confident the applicant *wants* to come to work for you and is willing to take the price you're willing to pay (or something close to it).

It used to be that employers took for granted that the employee worked for and at the employer's convenience. In some states, that employment-at-will philosophy still has a friend in the courts, but in many others, the idea has withered and died. Many managers now recognize that employees and employers work for and at the convenience of one another, which is why you have to sell the job, the organization, and *yourself* to the candidate. Working together is a shared responsibility established by a *psychological* contract, if not by an explicit or express contract.

You start building the psychological contract, which consists of the expectations you have of one another, during the exchange. You establish your expectations if the applicant were to become your employee, such as acceptable job performance, work-related attitudes and work-related behavior. At the same time, you let the other person know what he or she can expect from you: fair and equitable income, training, friendly supervision, performance review, and so forth. Letting the applicant establish some of these norms helps create the trust and confidence you two will have in each other. What happens during the exchange will affect your relationship throughout the applicant's career with you.

Another short dialogue illustrates how the exchange works:

Carl: I'm sure you have some questions for me, too.

Georgia: I do, and I've made some notes from some of the research I've done—in Moody's and Dun and Bradstreet. Mind if I use them?

Carl: No. Not at all.

Georgia: The company's net income last year was lower than it was the two previous years. I was wondering what that means.

Carl: We had an extraordinary expense last year, that's all. A major capital investment for which we paid cash. A new mainframe computer.

Georgia: You paid cash?

Carl: Right. As you've probably seen, we have no long-term debt at all. We either have the cash for making a capital investment or we don't make it.

Georgia: That's very interesting, but wouldn't it seem more equitable to the employees to put some of that cash into a profit-sharing or pension plan?

Carl: We have both, and we make decisions such as the one we made last year only after getting input from the troops. We surveyed the organization, and a new mainframe came out highest on the wish list. We couldn't handle the workload without it.

Georgia: Well, then, I'd like to know more about the profit-sharing and pension plans—and polling "the troops" seems to be very unique to your organization.

Carl: We like to think it is. About the profit-sharing and pension plans. . . .

You get the point. Openness, candor, friendliness—these are the norms Carl establishes at the very outset.

And Georgia was prepared (rather than prepped). All these qualities define the conditions in the psychological contract that Carl and the organization will try to reinforce from the start.

Studies have shown that the most important time for creating loyalty and dedication among new employees is during the *first three days* they are on the job. During those three days, the organization creates its most enduring impressions. No matter how long an employee stays with you, those impressions hang on forever.

The Close

Now you're ready to close—but without making any commitments. Even if you like a particular person—or in Carl's old words: even if he or she "seems like such a nice kid"—give yourself a chance to think about it. Often, a quick decision comes from the *"halo effect."*

During an interview, the candidate puts on his or her best front, just as you do. The applicant looks good partly because he or she is playing a role: job candidate. The candidate has said or done all the right things, otherwise he or she wouldn't have come this far. Now how can you turn away such an angel?

Well, you don't, but you don't hire this angel right now, either. He or she studied and rehearsed a large part of those *right* responses. The person behind the role has not been wholly visible. But then again, the real you hasn't been wholly visible either.

At this point, you find out if he or she wants to come back for another interview, talk briefly with you again, and meet with other people. If he or she's interested in pursuing the whole process (in spite of the fact you haven't made a specific offer), then you have a chance at getting this person.

Don't let anyone railroad you into making a decision with, "Well I need to know if you want to hire me. I have another opportunity, and have to give them an answer by tomorrow." You can probably guess at the appropriate response to that.

You'll want several opinions. (In some quarters, interview-by-committee has become popular.) Since the employee lives on the job with other people, too—other managers as well as his or her peers—you should take a look at how these potential coworkers react to him or her. Halos tarnish quickly under other people's scrutiny.

Yet, it's still your decision to make, and for you to make the best decision, you should see at least three candidates. Sometimes, because of a phenomenon called recency, the last person you see appears best of all. If it turns out that your third applicant does seem to be the best, add a fourth or call back the first to compare against the one with the shining halo. Then, and only then, should you see your best candidate again.

Let's peek in on Carl and Georgia again as Carl closes:

Carl: What else do you want to know about the job, about the organization, or even about me?

Georgia: I can't think of anything more. You've answered all the questions I brought with me—and then some. I appreciate your time.

Carl: It's been important to me, too. Well, then, let me ask you this. Frankly, what do you think about working here? [Open-ended trial close]

Georgia: I think I'd like to. What do *you* think about *me* working here?

Carl: You seem like the kind of person we want to hire, but, I can't make a decision until I've finished my interviews. In the meantime, I'd like you to meet some of the people with whom you will be working if we do hire you. Can you visit with them next Wednesday or Thursday?

Georgia: [*Checking her calendar*] Yes, I can. Either day—

Carl may just have himself a winner here, but that, too, is enough of that.

The Aftermath

I said earlier that you shouldn't take notes. Notetaking interferes with concentration, and it breaks the eye contact between you and the candidate. *Not* taking notes during the conversation gives the candidate your undivided attention and shows respect for what he or she is saying. Besides, you'll retain more than you think. If you're very concerned about retention, leave a margin in your interview guide for jotting down "cue" words or phrases that will help your recall.

Set aside enough time *after* the interview for writing up your notes as soon as the candidate leaves. Don't share them with anyone with whom the applicant will interview until after you get the other interviewer's opinion. You don't want to program him or her.

After you've seen everyone you're going to see, if the other opinions are positive, call the candidate back in for a hiring interview.

Chapter 6

A Few Words on the Hiring Interview

During the hiring interview, you're mainly negotiating price, and it shouldn't take long. Since you're buying, you need to find out just how badly that person wants to sell. Unless you have only one price to offer, be prepared to bargain.

It's a good practice to know going in how much the applicant wants and start your offers somewhere below it. Most employment applications ask for the desired starting salary, but it's a good idea to ask anyway. Don't, however, ask, "How much are you willing to work for?" or "How much do you want?" A much better question is, "Bottom line—rent, food, clothing, bills—how much do you really need to live?" The answer to that question is usually lower than what you're prepared to offer, and it makes your offer seem large in comparison.

Here is the final episode of "Carl and Georgia Make a Deal":

Carl: You impressed everyone with whom you spoke.

Georgia: Thank you. That makes me feel good.

Carl: Would you like to come to work with us?

Georgia: I was hoping you'd ask. I said in my note thanking you for the interview that this job is the most interesting of the three for which I've interviewed.

Carl: Now, that makes *me* feel good. So, Georgia, can you start on the first?

Georgia: Yes I can, but— I— That is—

Carl: Yes, I know, we haven't discussed salary yet. Bottom line—rent, food, clothing, bills—how much do you really need to live?

Georgia: I hadn't stopped to think about it like that, but adding in gas money, I guess around $1,200 a month. But that's what I'm making now. I'm not looking for bottom line.

Carl: I know you're not. No one I know is. We're able to pay $1,400 a month to start, with a salary review in six months and a second one on your one-year anniversary date. How does that sound to you?

Georgia: That's better than bottom line—

By checking her salary wants, Carl found out what she was making, and he knew he had room to negotiate. Although he could have offered more, he's bringing her in below the midpoint in her pay range. That gives him somewhere to go with her income in six months, and again in twelve. Without that room to maneuver, he'd have no way to provide first-year salary *incentives.* If your company permits that type of negotiation, we recommend you do the same as Carl did.

Conclusion

Well, that's it! The effective way to interview another person consists largely of sound, rational planning. Asking the right questions in the right way for the purpose of making the right decision.

Preparation takes a lot of time at the front end and seems costly, but consider the cost of not preparing. Improvised, spontaneous, unrehearsed interviews cost Carl time, money, professional status, and a decent night's sleep. I think you'll prefer the payoff from preparation instead of the one you get from its opposite.

And take the time to interview properly. Don't rush it. Set aside the time you need, both during and afterward, to find out and mull over all you can about the person's work history, education and training, and personal traits. Don't short-change yourself in this department. You may have to take at least two hours to talk with each likely candidate.

Follow the four steps: (1) openers, (2) inquiry, (3) exchange, and (4) close, and use the tools discussed—the questions and the comments.

When you have other people available to check your opinion, show them your interview guide (but not the answers) so they can look for some of the same things you did. See if they find a halo too. If they do, you can strike a deal with the candidate.

Be prepared to negotiate. A prime candidate for a prime job may present more of challenge than Georgia did. You may have to play hardball with a star in your profession. But even a star is open to reaching an accommodation with someone for whom he or she has respect and with whom he or she wants to work. What else can anyone ask for?

Appendix

Job Analysis Worksheet

INSTRUCTIONS: (1) Begin each task name with an action verb; (2) keep task names short; (3) list tasks taking the most time first; (4) in #/Hours, put down how often and how much time in hours each task takes.

D = Daily   **W** = Weekly   **M** = Monthly

Job Title: _____ Department/Unit: _____

Objectives: _____

_____

Job Qualifications: _____

_____

| # | TASKS | Frequency/Estimated Time | | | | |
		D	W	M	Other	#/Hours

Task Analysis Worksheet

INSTRUCTIONS: (1) List one task name at a time in order of importance; (2) list skills needed for doing each task in order of importance.

E = Essential   **I** = Important   **N** = Nice to have

Job Title _____

Department/Unit _____

#	TASKS/SKILLS	IMPORTANCE

#	TASKS/SKILLS	IMPORTANCE

Interview Guide Worksheet

INSTRUCTIONS: (1) Using your job and task analyses, complete each item needed on the left-hand side of the T-chart; (2) on the right-hand side, list questions to ask. Use the candidate's résumé or application to ask specific questions about his or her background. Use the sample in Exhibit 3 as a guide, but don't let the number of questions in the sample limit you. Use extra pages.

POSITION SPECIFICATIONS	INTERVIEW GUIDE

INDEX

About the Author

Donald H. Weiss, Ph.D., of Millers' Mutual Insurance in Alton, Illinois, has been engaged in education and training for over twenty-six years and has written numerous articles, books, audiocassette/workbook programs, and video training films on effective sales and supervisory or management skills. As a Certified Personnel Consultant, Dr. Weiss speaks regularly on stress management and other personal development subjects, and has produced a variety of related printed or recorded materials.

During his career, Dr. Weiss has been the Manager of Special Projects for a training and development firm, the Manager of Management Training for an insurance company, the Director of Training for an employment agency group, a training consultant, and a writer-producer-director of video training tapes. He also has taught at several universities and colleges in Texas, including the University of Texas at Arlington and Texas Christian University in Fort Worth.

Currently, Dr. Weiss is Corporate Training Director for Millers' Mutual Insurance.